OUR AMAZING WORLD

HORSES

Kay de Silva

Aurora

Contents

A mare in a field at dawn.

HORSES

A horse is one of the most beautiful of all mammals. It has a strong body, long legs, and hooves. These help it to run fast. A horse can also travel long distances without getting tired.

A strong Bay Horse rearing up.

ANATOMY

A horse has a strong body. A fully grown horse can weigh up to 1,000 pounds (455kg). It has 175 bones in its body. Most horse breeds have 17 ribs in their bodies. The Arabian horse has 18. Horses have different colors and markings. In winter a horse grows a thicker coat to protect it from the cold.

A close-up of horses' hooves.

LEGS & HOOVES

A horse has powerful legs. This is why it can run for a long time. It can gallop at a speed of 44 kilometres per hour (27 miles per hour) and for long distances without stopping.

A horse's hooves bear the weight of its limbs, so it is important that its hooves are healthy. A horse hoof grows about 1 centimetre every month. Domestic horses wear horse shoes. They help to keep the hoofs from wearing off. These shoes need to be changed every 6 to 8 weeks.

MANE

Horses have magnificent hair. The mane is the hair that grows from the top of the neck to the withers (where a horse's neck meets its back). It is thicker than the rest of the horse's coat. Its mane is almost like human hair but three times as thick.

A horse's mane grows to cover its neck. The mane is said to keep the horse's neck warm. It helps keep water off its neck if it cannot get shelter from the rain. It also helps keep away flies.

A snow-white stallion with a luscious mane.

TAIL

A horse's tail is most useful to chase away flies. Some horses have tails so long they almost touch the ground. The horse also uses its tail to talk to other horses. Tail up says go. Tail down says stop. Beware when a horse swishes its tail from side to side. It means that it is ready to kick!

A smart Tinker Horse with a full mane and tail.

Eye of an Arabian horse.

EYES

A horse has large, wide-set eyes. Its eyes are the largest of all land mammals. They are located on either side of its head. It can see almost everything around. What it cannot see is what is on its back and directly below. This is why its sense of smell is very important.

A horse alert and listening.

HEARING

A horse has very sensitive hearing. It does not like loud noises. If you approach a horse you should speak softly. This tells it that you are a friend.

Movement of its long ears shows you how it feels. Tilting one of its ears means it is listening. Both ears pinned flat to its head means that it is angry. When both ears are perked forward, it means there is danger.

Horses meet and greet.

SMELL

A horse likes to use its nose. It tries to smell every object it approaches. Horses recognise each other by their smell. They also greet each other nose to nose. In this way they take in the odor of the other.

A horse can smell a hundred times better than we can! If you happen to approach a horse, first let it smell the back of your hand. Keep your hand outstretched as you slowly walk towards it. This way it will know you are a friend.

Horses nuzzle, scratch, and lick to show affection.

TOUCH

Horses are very sensitive to touch. They scratch other horses with their teeth if they are friends. You can tell a horse that you are a friend by scratching it in places it cannot reach, such as its withers. If it thinks you are a friend, it will scratch you with its teeth! This is how horses show affection.

Two horses having a chat.

SPEECH

A horse makes different sounds. The loudest sound it makes is a neigh.
A neigh is a long, high-pitched sound. A horse neighs when it feels brave.
It neighs in battle. It also neighs when it looks for other horses. It is as if it is
saying, *Where are you guys? I am here!*

When a horse is in danger, it snorts. It sometimes snorts when it is excited.
A horse also nickers. This is a soft sound a horse makes with its mouth closed.
It means hello, how are you? And when a horse is relaxed and comfortable,
it may let out a long sigh.

(L-R) The Grey Shire is much taller than a human. The pony is smaller than the child.

HEIGHT

Horses vary in height. Some are taller than humans. Others are shorter.
A horse's height is measured in hands. A hand equals four inches
(10 centimeters). A horse's height is measured from the ground to its withers.
The neck and the head are not included in the measurement. This is because
a horse moves its head and neck a lot.

WALK

TROT

GALLOP

Computer simulated images of the natural gaits of a horse.

GAIT

The way a horse moves is called its *gait*. All horses have 4 natural gaits. The *walk* is the slowest. The *trot* is a bit faster. It is equal to the speed that most people jog. The canter is faster than the trot. The *gallop* is the fastest. You see horses galloping at races. In the wild, horses gallop to escape preda-tors.

Other gaits such as the *amble gait* can be done by a few horses. Other horses need to be trained in these gaits.

Horses sharing a meal and a drink.

DIET

A horse is an *herbivore*. This means that it eats grass and other plants. It does not eat meat. It uses its whiskers to find suitable food to eat. It uses its lips and front teeth to filter its food. Unlike most people who eat three big meals every day, a horse eats constantly. It may also need to drink as much as 10 gallons of water each day.

FAMILY

A baby horse is called a *foal*. When it turns 6 months it is called a *yearling*. Between the ages of 2 and 4 years a male horse is called a *colt*. A female is called a *filly*. A grown male is called a *stallion* and a female a *mare*.

A group of horses is called a *herd*. Each member of the herd has a role. The strongest male is called the *lead stallion*. Its partner is called the *alpha mare*. A horse feels safe in a herd. If a horse is not part of a herd, it becomes sad and lonely.

A herd of horses headed by a lead stallion.

A baby foal finds its mummy.

BABY HORSES

A foal is usually born at night during springtime. It can run shortly after its birth. Like all mammals, it first drinks milk from its mother.

A foal cannot eat grass because it cannot reach the ground. Some members of the herd are in charge of looking after the foals. They are called *guardians*.

A guardian watching over a sleeping foal.

SLEEP

A horse is always alert, so it often sleeps standing up. It lies down to rest for only 45 minutes a day. When a horse lies down to sleep, others in the herd keep watch. They remain standing or in a light

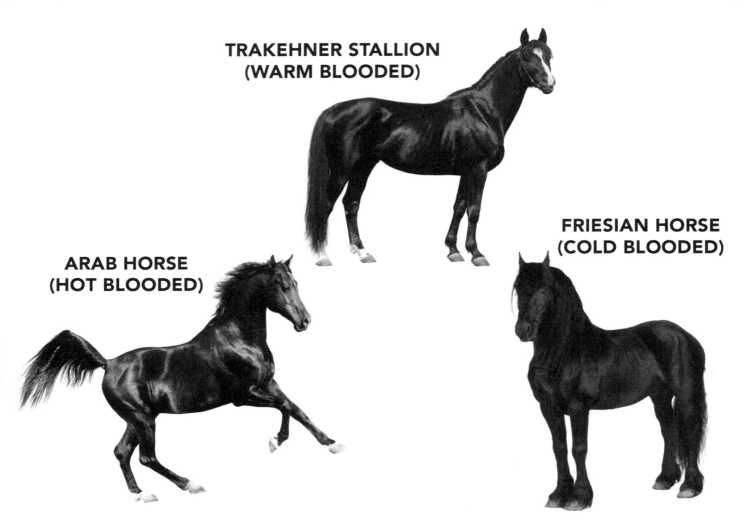

**TRAKEHNER STALLION
(WARM BLOODED)**

**FRIESIAN HORSE
(COLD BLOODED)**

**ARAB HORSE
(HOT BLOODED)**

Horse temperaments by breed.

TEMPERAMENT

A horse can have different temperaments. It can be *hot blooded*, *warm blooded*, or *cold blooded*. A hot blooded horse is often fast and has lots of energy. It is quick to learn. It has long legs and thick skin. It is often used in races.

A warm blooded horse is calmer and bigger than a hot blooded horse. It is used as a riding horse.

A cold blooded horse is the most muscular and the heaviest of horses. It is also the calmest. It is known as a *gentle giant*.

A beautiful Arabian Horse in motion.

ARABIAN HORSES

The *Arabian* or *Arab Horse* is one of the oldest breeds. It comes from countries with deserts. Be-cause of this it can live in very hot and very cold climates. An Arab horse can live with very little food.

An Arabian horse is hot blooded. It is sensitive, alert, and willing to learn. It is also quick to learn, which makes this horse valuable. Some desert people let their horses stay in the family tent to keep them safe. At times when there is not enough water they are given camel's milk.

A close-up of a gorgeous Palomino Draft horse.

DRAFT HORSES

A *Draft Horse* is a breed that is used for work. It is a cold-blooded horse, which means it is gentle and calm. It is also called a *Work Horse* or *Heavy Horse*. It is large and strong. Because of this, it is used on farms for heavy labour and to plough the field.

A Mustang stallion confrontation: Who will lead the herd?

FERAL HORSES

A *Feral Horse* is a free-roaming horse. Although it lives in the wild, it is different from a *Wild Horse*. A Feral horse has ancestors that were once domesticated. Its ancestors probably strayed, es-caped, or were released to the wild. After that, they lived and had families in the wilderness.

A *Mustang* is a *Feral Horse* that is mostly found in America. Australia has the largest Feral horse population in the world. There are about 400,000 of them in the wild. They are called *Brumby*. They are descendants of horses brought to Australia by English settlers.

A Norwegian Fjord mare and colt.

NORWEGIAN FJORDS

The *Norwegian Fjord Horse* is small for a horse, but is very strong. It is friendly and good-tempered. Like the Arab Horse, it is an old breed. This horse is from the mountainous regions of Western Norway. For hundreds of years, farmers in Norway have used it as a companion in the field.

The Fjord Horse was known as the horse of the Vikings. Drawings of the Fjord Horse can be found on Viking rune stones. It has been a tradition to trim the mane of this horse so that it stands up. This is to shows off its strong neck.

A horse and pony running in a paddock.

HORSES AND PONIES

A *Pony* is not a baby horse. It is an adult horse that is smaller in size. Any horse under 14.2 hands is considered to be a Pony. It often has a stocky body and shorter legs. Its neck is shorter than a horse's. Its ears are also smaller. It has a thicker coat, mane, and tail.

A Pony is very strong. Some Ponies can pull as much as 4-1/2 times their own weight. Because it has a thicker coat, a Pony is more suited for winter when compared to a horse. Countries with harsh climates rely on the Pony to do hard work. It eats less than a horse does and does not need much variety when it comes to food. It also lives longer than a horse.

The most well-known Pony is from the *Shetland Isles* in the United Kingdon and is called the *Shetland Pony*. It is the strongest of all ponies and horse breeds. It also lives longer.

A portrait of a Thoroughbred Horse.

THOROUGHBRED HORSES

The *Thoroughbred* is a hot blooded horse. It is fast, agile, and easily excitable. It is often used for horse racing. Its height ranges from 15 to 17 hands. It comes in various colors. These include bay, seal, brown, chestnut black, and grey. The best Thoroughbred horse has a long neck, a short back, a lean body, and long legs.

All Thoroughbreds have the same birthday, no matter on which day of the year they are born. In the Northern hemisphere their birthday is celebrated on the first of January. In the Southern hemisphere it is celebrated on the first of August. This makes record keeping easy for horse owners.

A pair of Przewalski Horses in the wilderness.

WILD HORSES

A *Wild Horse* is a horse that has never been tamed. There were two species of Wild horses: the *Tarpan* and the *Przewalski*. The Tarpan was the ancestor of most domesticated horses, but is now ex-tinct.

The Przewalski is also known as the *Asian Wild Horse*. It is an *endangered species*. It was once al-most extinct in the wild. There was a time when only 9 were left in captivity. They were bred in zoos and reintroduced to the wild. Now there are about 300 in the wild.

HORSE AND MAN

Horse and man have been friends for a very long time. Horses are used to carry people from place to place. People ride horses either *bareback* or using a *saddle*. Before there were cars, horses were used to draw carriages. Horses were also used in battle.

Horses were first domesticated around 4000 BC in Central Asia. That is over 6,000 years ago. Horses were smaller then. They were kept for their milk and as food. People did not ride them at the time. Instead, they were used for pulling carriages, carts, chariots, and ploughs.

It was only about 1,000 years later that horses were big enough to be ridden. They were eventually used in warfare. Today, domesticated horses play a role in work, sport, and entertainment.

Domestic Horses live in stables or barns. They depend on people to provide them shelter. They also live in pastures protected by fences. Some horses have very fancy barns, but horses do not really care. They are happy as long as there is food, water, and space.

Child feeding a horse.

Horses galloping at sunset.

HORSES AND NATURE

Wild horses and Feral horses live on their own. Nature provides everything that they need. Because of pollution, however, their homes are slowly being destroyed. Soon, there will not be enough green and open space where horses can freely run around. To protect horses, we must be kind to nature and protect our environment.

OUR AMAZING WORLD
COLLECT THEM ALL

WWW.OURAMAZINGWORLDBOOKS.COM

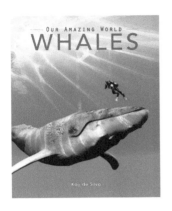

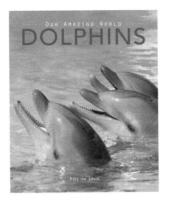

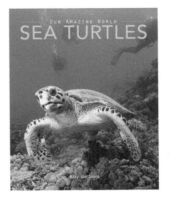

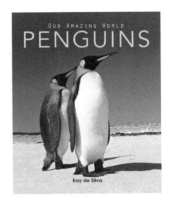

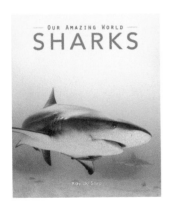

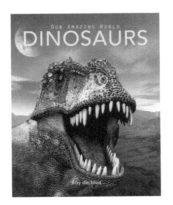

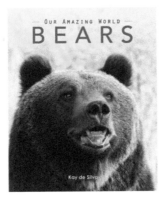

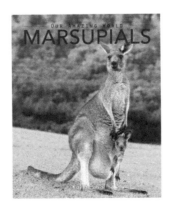

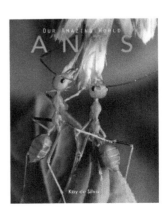

Aurora
An imprint of CKTY Publishing Solutions

ouramazingworldbooks.com

Text copyright © Kay de Silva, 2013
The moral right of the author has been asserted

ISBN 978-0-9946009-2-9

shutterstock.com